The Satanic Market: 2019

Created by George A. Hart

© George A. Hart 2019. No part of The Satanic Market may be reproduced without prior written consent from the publisher or copyright holders.

ISBN: 978-1-943287-03-1

The Satanic Market
http://thesatanicmarket.com
George A. Hart Publishing
https://gh-publishing.com
ghpublish@gmail.com
732-552-6991

The Satanic Market
The Annual Book For Your Products and Websites

Table of Contents

Websites	*5*
Books	*11*
Clothing	*29*
Music CDs	*49*
Accessories	*53*

Websites

Your Ad. Title

This could be your ad.!

The Satanic Market, is an annual bookazine where you can place all of your Satanic Advertisements.

$10 Full Page Ad.

$10 full page ad. placement.
$100 ad. creation.

http://thesatanicmarket.com

ghpublish@gmail.com

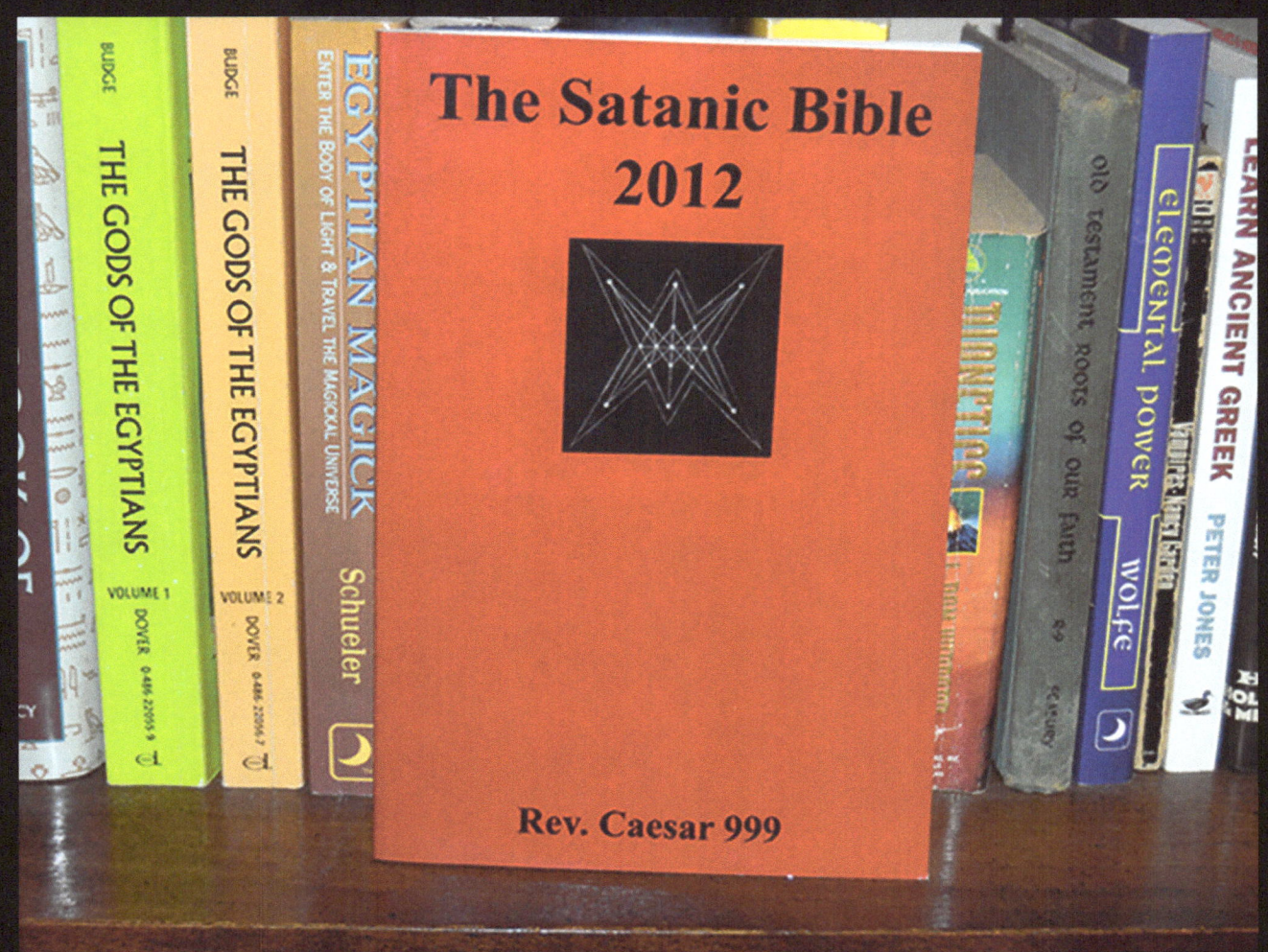

The Satanic Bible 2012 by Rev. Caesar 999

George A. Hart Publishing

*Publish your Satanic Book for $200
and receive 80% of royalties.*

http://gh-publishing.com

https://georgeahartpublishing.com

Church of The Antichrist 999
Temple of Satanic Kali

High Priest Caesar 999 created Spiritual Satanism 999, founded the underground Church of The Antichrist 999, and Temple of Satanic Kali.

In an effort to spread his religion and temple the costs of running websites, printing books, and advertising has led to asking our supporters to become members, pay memberships, buy his books, and donate when possible!

Also, members are expected to become, Tantric Priests, Tantric Priestesses, Warrior-Priests, Warrior-Priestesses, and Satanic Models!

Membership is $10 per year!
Members will have access to the following benefits:
Member List, Chat Rooms,
Private Chat, Video Chat, Photo Gallery, etc.

This website is for those 18+ and contains nudity and sexuality!
https://churchoftheantichrist999.com

Satanic Models

Satanic Models offer semi and full nude photos, videos, and webcam performing!

Currently, as an example for a 1 hour private session it costs $100 and for a 30 minute private session it costs $50!

http://satanicmodels.com

Your Ad. Title

This could be your ad.!

The Satanic Market, is an annual bookazine where you can place all of your Satanic Advertisements.

$10 Full Page Ad.

$10 full page ad. placement.
$100 ad. creation.

http://thesatanicmarket.com

ghpublish@gmail.com

Books

Your Ad. Title

This could be your ad.!

The Satanic Market, is an annual bookazine where you can place all of your Satanic Advertisements.

$10 Full Page Ad.

$10 full page ad. placement.
$100 ad. creation.

http://thesatanicmarket.com

ghpublish@gmail.com

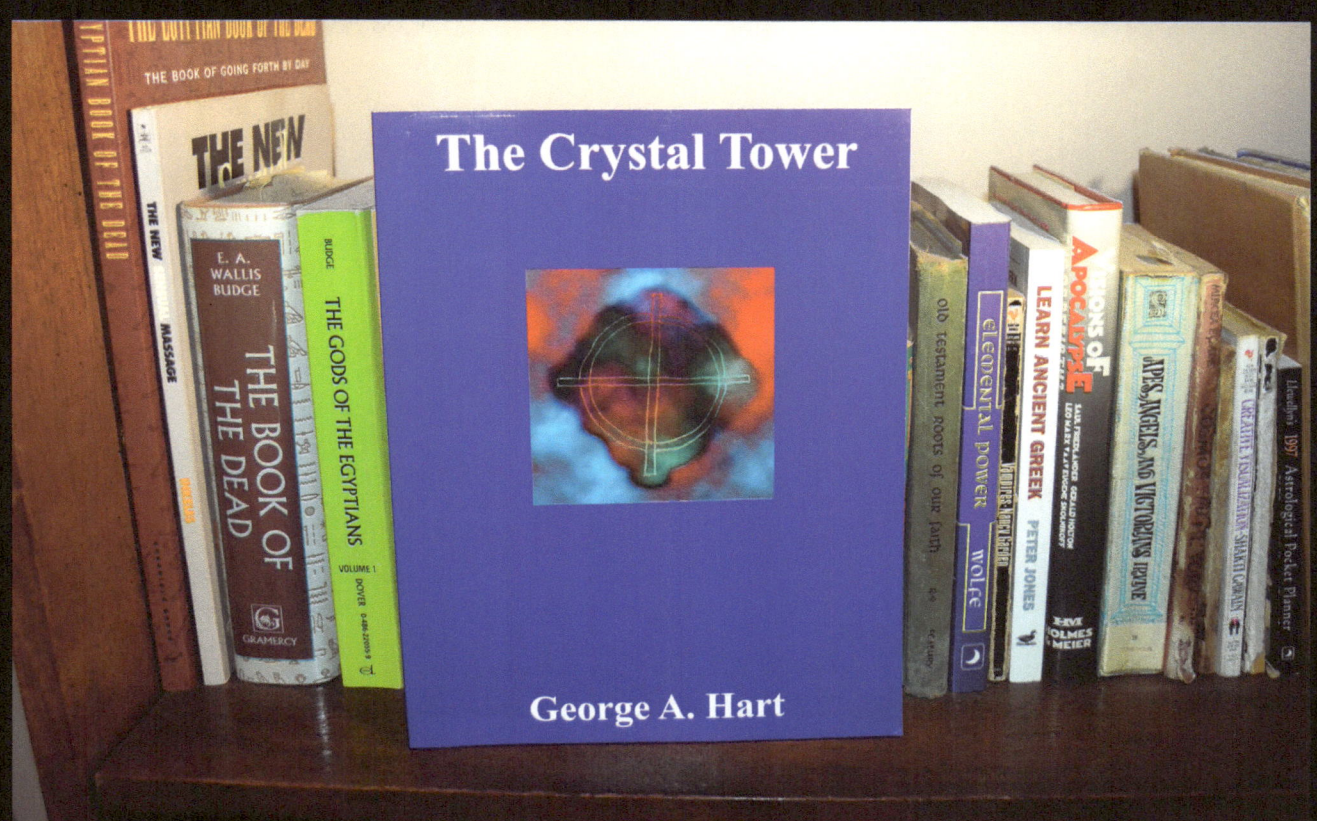

The Crystal Tower
by
George A. Hart

https://georgeahartpublishing.com

George A. Hart Publishing Shop

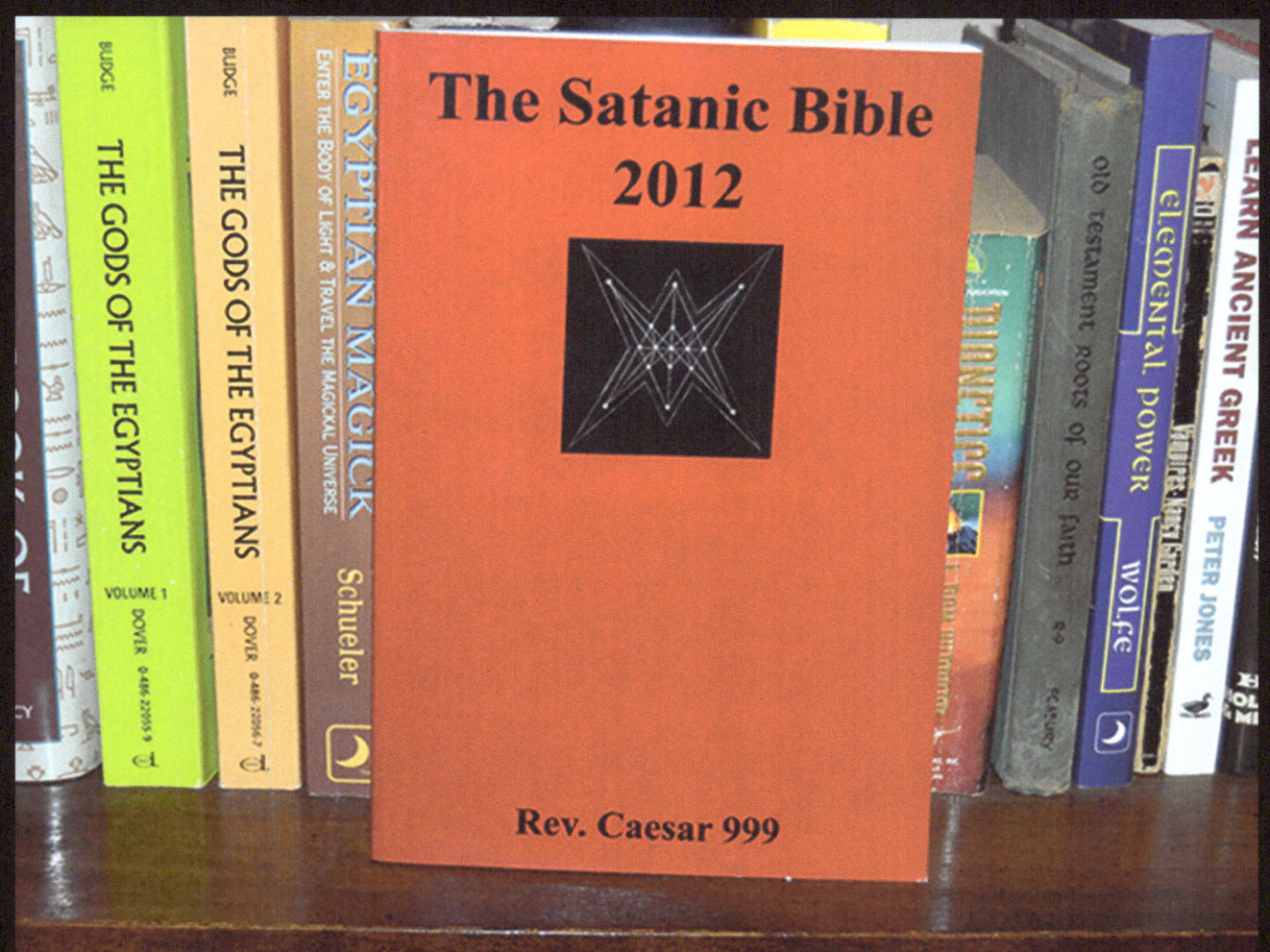

The Satanic Bible 2012 by Rev. Caesar 999

When true Spirituality combines with a
naturally Anti-christian Carnal Philosophy,
a new religion is born!
Buy The Satanic Bible 2012,
to learn about Spiritual Satanism 999.

The Satanic Bible
by
Rev. Caesar 999

https://georgeahartpublishing.com
George A. Hart Publishing Shop

Satan's Sorcery Volume I: The Eye of Satan

By

Rev. Caesar 999

http://georgeahartpublishing.com
George A. Hart Publishing Shop

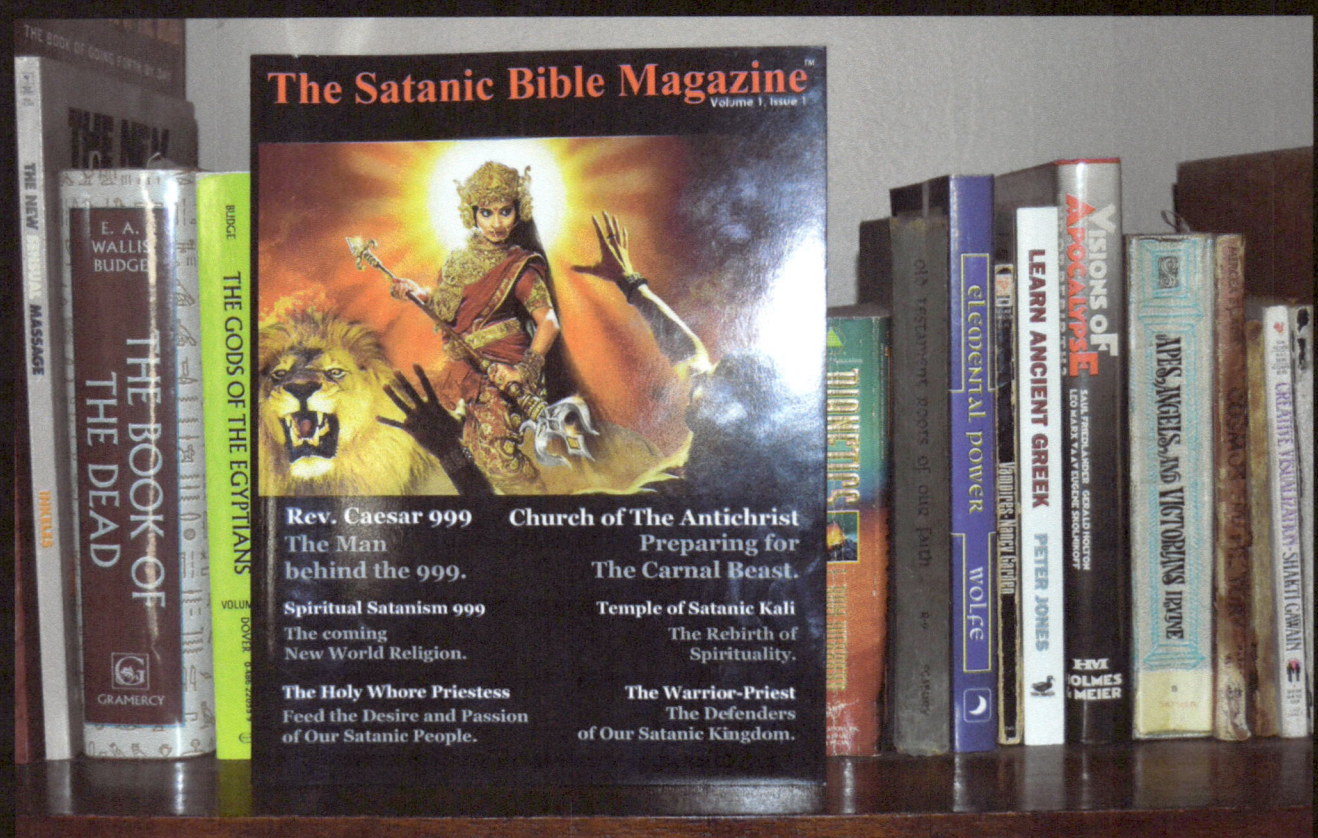

The Satanic Bible Magazine
Created by George A. Hart

https://georgeahartpublishing.com
George A. Hart Publishing Shop

The Tantric Hindu Bible: Eastern Satanism

Rev. Caesar 999

The Shadow Garden
By
George A. Hart

https://georgeahartpublishing.com
George A. Hart Publishing Shop

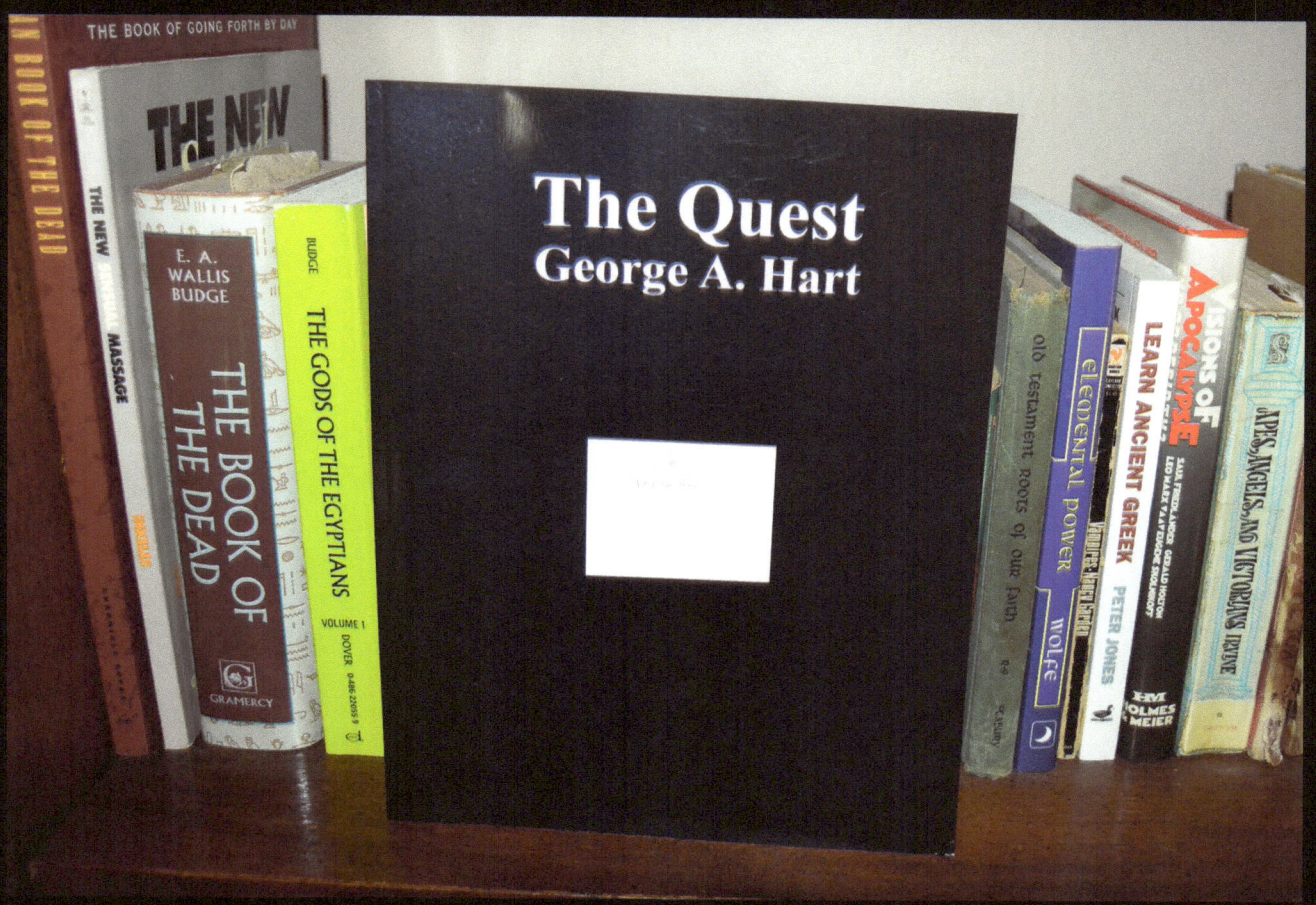

The Quest
By
George A. Hart

https://georgeahartpublishing.com

George A. Hart Publishing Shop

Welcome To Zone X
By
George A. Hart
https://georgeahartpublishing.com
George A. Hart Publishing Shop

Heaven on Earth

by

George A. Hart

Your Ad. Title

This could be your ad.!

The Satanic Market, is an annual bookazine where you can place all of your Satanic Advertisements.

$10 Full Page Ad.

$10 full page ad. placement.
$100 ad. creation.

http://thesatanicmarket.com

ghpublish@gmail.com

Clothing

Your Ad. Title

This could be your ad.!

The Satanic Market, is an annual bookazine where you can place all of your Satanic Advertisements.

$10 Full Page Ad.

$10 full page ad. placement.
$100 ad. creation.

http://thesatanicmarket.com

ghpublish@gmail.com

Church of the Antichrist 999
Men's T-Shirt
C.O.T.A. 999 - Red Blood Letters
$25.00

https://georgeahartpublishing.com

George A. Hart Publishing Shop

Church of the Antichrist 999
Women's T-Shirt
C.O.T.A. 999 - Red Blood Letters
$25.00

https://georgeahartpublishing.com

George A. Hart Publishing Shop

**Temple of Satanic Kali
Men's T-Shirt
T.O.S.K. - Red Blood Letters
$25.00**

**https://georgeahartpublishing.com
George A. Hart Publishing Shop**

**Temple of Satanic Kali
Women's T-Shirt
T.O.S.K. - Red Blood Letters
$25.00**

**https://georgeahartpublishing.com
George A. Hart Publishing Shop**

Satanic Models
Men's T-Shirt
Red Blood Letters
$25.00

https://georgeahartpublishing.com
George A. Hart Publishing Shop

Satanic Models
Women's T-Shirt
Red Blood Letters
$25.00

https://georgeahartpublishing.com
George A. Hart Publishing Shop

George's Barn
You are part of the legend!
Men's T-Shirt
$25.00

https://georgeahartpublishing.com
George A. Hart Publishing Shop

George's Barn
You are part of the legend!
Women's T-Shirt
$25.00

https://georgeahartpublishing.com
George A. Hart Publishing Shop

George's Barn
You are part of the legend!
Men's T-Shirt - Long Sleeve
$30.00

https://georgeahartpublishing.com
George A. Hart Publishing Shop

George's Barn
You are part of the legend!
Women's T-Shirt - Long Sleeve
$30.00

https://georgeahartpublishing.com
George A. Hart Publishing Shop

George's Barn
You are part of the legend!
Unisex Fleece Zip Hoodie
$49.00

https://georgeahartpublishing.com
George A. Hart Publishing Shop

George's Barn
You are part of the legend!
Unisex Fleece Zip Hoodie
Larger Banner - $49.00

https://georgeahartpublishing.com
George A. Hart Publishing Shop

George's Barn
You are part of the legend!
Men's Zip Hoodie
Largest Banner - $49.00

https://georgeahartpublishing.com
George A. Hart Publishing Shop

Church of the Antichrist 999 Women's T-Shirt C.O.T.A. 999 - White Letters $25.00

https://georgeahartpublishing.com

George A. Hart Publishing Shop

Satanic Models
Unisex Fleece Zip Hoodie
Red Blood Letters
$55.00

https://georgeahartpublishing.com
George A. Hart Publishing Shop

Satanic Models
Unisex Fleece Zip Hoodie
White Letters
$55.00

https://georgeahartpublishing.com
George A. Hart Publishing Shop

Satanic Models
Men's Pullover Hoodie
White Letters
$40.00

https://georgeahartpublishing.com
George A. Hart Publishing Shop

Satanic Models
Unisex Fleece Zip Hoodie
White Blood Letters
$55.00

https://georgeahartpublishing.com
George A. Hart Publishing Shop

Music CDs

Your Ad. Title

This could be your ad.!

The Satanic Market, is an annual bookazine where you can place all of your Satanic Advertisements.

$10 Full Page Ad.

$10 full page ad. placement.
$100 ad. creation.

http://thesatanicmarket.com

ghpublish@gmail.com

Rev. Caesar 999

Ritual Songs & Poems Volume I

Rev. Caesar 999
Ritual Songs & Poems
Volume I - $20.00

https://georgeahartpublishing.com
George A. Hart Publishing Shop

Rev. Caesar 999

Rituals Songs & Poems Volume II

Rev. Caesar 999
Ritual Songs & Poems
Volume II - $20.00

https://georgeahartpublishing.com
George A. Hart Publishing Shop

Accessories

Your Ad. Title

This could be your ad.!

The Satanic Market, is an annual bookazine where you can place all of your Satanic Advertisements.

$10 Full Page Ad.

$10 full page ad. placement.
$100 ad. creation.

http://thesatanicmarket.com

ghpublish@gmail.com

Satanic Models
Knit Hat
Red Blood Letters - $24.00

https://georgeahartpublishing.com
George A. Hart Publishing Shop

Satanic Models
Knit Hat
White Letters - $24.00

https://georgeahartpublishing.com
George A. Hart Publishing Shop

**Satanic Models
Duffel Bag
Red Blood Letters - $35.00**

**https://georgeahartpublishing.com
George A. Hart Publishing Shop**

Satanic Models
Duffel Bag
White Letters - $35.00

https://georgeahartpublishing.com
George A. Hart Publishing Shop

Your Ad. Title

This could be your ad.!

The Satanic Market, is an annual bookazine where you can place all of your Satanic Advertisements.

$10 Full Page Ad.

$10 full page ad. placement.
$100 ad. creation.

http://thesatanicmarket.com

ghpublish@gmail.com